LAFAYETTE

FRIEND OF AMERICAN LIBERTY

Lafayette

LAFAYETTE

THE FRIEND OF AMERICAN LIBERTY

BY

ALMA HOLMAN BURTON

YESTERDAY'S CLASSICS

ITHACA, NEW YORK

ISBN: 978-1-59915-363-6

Yesterday's Classics, LLC
PO Box 339
Ithaca, NY 14851

INTRODUCTION

The story of the Marquis de Lafayette forms one of the most interesting chapters in the history of human liberty. To understand clearly the nature of Lafayette's services, both to America and to the whole world, we must first think of the conditions of life at the beginning of his career, and then contrast them with those which now prevail. One hundred and forty years ago, when Lafayette was a child, the world was not so pleasant a place to live in as it is in our own time. Even in the most enlightened countries of Europe, the majority of the people were downtrodden and oppressed. Men had scarcely so much as heard of liberty. Outside of England and her colonies, the idea of popular freedom was unknown.

This idea, as you may have learned elsewhere, seems to have been a sort of birthright of the Anglo-Saxon race. Ever since the barons of England forced King John to grant them a charter of rights, the peoples of that race have defended and cherished it. Like a spark of fire in the midst of general gloom, it has oftentimes been almost extinguished; and yet, no matter how its enemies have tried to stamp it out, it has survived and been rekindled.

The American colonists, because this idea of liberty was implanted in their hearts, rebelled against the tyranny of George III, and boldly demanded their rights as freeborn Englishmen. Frenchmen, at that time, would not have done this. They would have tamely submitted to every form of oppression, not yet having learned that the common people have certain rights which even kings must respect. Indeed, at the very time that the American patriots were refusing to obey the unjust laws of their English rulers, the common people of France were suffering from oppressions ten times as great; and yet they had no thought of resistance, but submitted silently, as creatures whose only duty was to obey their masters. At the very time that our forefathers were resisting the payment of the tax on tea, the common people of France were paying all the taxes for the support of the French king and his nobles.

So burdensome were these taxes that they consumed the greater part of every man's earnings. The people had no voice in the management of public affairs, nor had they any rights save to toil unceasingly for those who had set themselves over them. Every year thousands of persons died of starvation, because the earnings of labor, instead of providing food for the laborers, were taken for taxes. Meanwhile, the nobles, or privileged classes, who owned all the land, were living in ease and luxury; they did no work of any kind; they paid no taxes; they seemed to live for no purpose but to gratify their own pleasures and do honor to the king.

Such was the condition of France at the time Lafayette was preparing to aid the cause of liberty in

America. Do you ask why he did not first help the oppressed in his own country? They were not yet ready to be profited by such assistance. The time was not ripe for any movement against the tyranny of the king and his court. To the downtrodden people of France, liberty seemed a thing so impossible that they had not even so much as dreamed of contending for it.

Lafayette was not one of the people—he was a member of the nobility, and we should naturally expect to find him arrayed on the side of the oppressor rather than on that of the oppressed. But here his patriotism seems all the more praiseworthy because it was wholly unselfish. What could he expect to gain by befriending the American colonists? They could not even offer him a salary as an officer in the continental army. Did he hope to win fame by great achievements in war? There were in Europe other and more promising fields for the display of military genius. In only one way can we account for his ardor in behalf of American liberty, and that is by saying that he was imbued with the true spirit of freedom, and was, therefore, a friend to all mankind. He thought that he saw in America the first opportunity to do good by striking a blow at oppression. The results were greater than any one could have dreamed. Without his aid it is hardly possible that our revolution would have succeeded; without it, the American colonies might have still remained under the control of Great Britain. But his friendship for American liberty turned the tide and made the history of the nineteenth century very different from what it would otherwise have been. The success of the American cause aroused the long-oppressed people of France to a sense of their rights and urged them to a similar resistance to tyranny. Thus, through lending aid to the colonists, Lafayette found the surest means of doing service for his own countrymen, and the people of two continents thereby became his debtors.

What has been the final result of these uprisings for liberty? The spirit of freedom has extended its blessed influence over the whole globe, and to-day there is hardly a country under the sun from which tyranny and oppression have not been banished. The right of every man to life, liberty, and the pursuit of happiness is no longer disputed; for men everywhere have learned the true meaning of liberty and have acquired the courage to stand up fearlessly in its defense.

To the great leaders, statesmen, and warriors, through whom American independence was won, the whole world owes a debt of gratitude. And, while every American citizen takes pleasure in commemorating the deeds of Washington, our greatest patriot, let the place next to him in our affections be reserved for that brave friend of American liberty, the Marquis de Lafayette.

JAMES BALDWIN

CONTENTS

CHAPTER I

THE COLONIES IN NORTH AMERICA

One hundred and fifty years ago North America was claimed by three kingdoms of Europe. Spain claimed Florida, Mexico, and the country west of the Rocky Mountains; France claimed Canada and the vast region between the Rocky Mountains and the Alleghenies; and England claimed a wide strip of land extending from the Gulf of St. Lawrence to Florida, and running

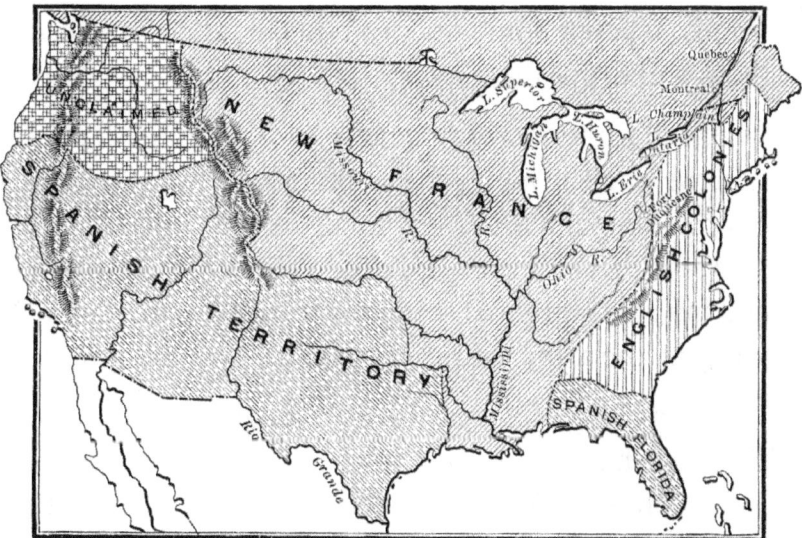

Our Country in 1750

1

straight through the territories of France and Spain, as far west as the Pacific Ocean.

Now Spain did not fear England's pretensions in the least. The Pacific slope was an unknown region beyond the Rocky Mountains, and no one dreamed that an Englishman would ever cross the trackless wilderness and climb those dizzy heights. But France knew very well that whenever the thirteen colonies along the Atlantic coast became densely settled, the English would try to seize the fertile valley of the Ohio. And so, while English colonists were cultivating farms and building towns east of the Allegheny Mountains, French soldiers were setting up a strong line of forts west of them.

At last, some English traders ventured across the mountains. They built rude huts, and were laying the foundations of a fort, where the city of Pittsburgh now stands, when a company of French soldiers attacked them and drove them away.

"Such impudence must be punished immediately," said the English; and General Braddock, with an army of British regulars, was sent to recover the fort. He met with sore defeat at the hands of the French and Indians, and but for George Washington, a young lieutenant of Virginia, the army would have been wholly destroyed.

Thus a long war began between England and France. The English conquered Canada, and because Spain had helped France in some European wars, they also seized the Spanish island of Cuba.

In 1763, envoys from France, England, and Spain met at Paris to sign a treaty of peace. They were very polite to one another, and took a great deal of snuff, after the fashion of the time; but, for all that, each envoy was determined to get the best terms for his king that he could.

In the end, the map of the New World was greatly altered. England had exchanged Cuba for Florida, while France had ceded Canada and the country between the Mississippi River and the Allegheny Mountains to England, and all west of the Mississippi to Spain.

This treaty of Paris gave to England and Spain the exclusive ownership of North America. There was not a foot of the land which the French could call their own.

The king of France grieved over the loss of his possessions. He said he hoped the thirteen colonies would prove so unruly that the English king would wish the French back in Canada to help keep them in subjection.

George III

Now, if George III of England had proved to be a good and worthy king, perhaps this hope would never have been realized. At the beginning of his reign, his colonies were prosperous and contented. They celebrated his birthdays, set up his statues in public parks, and offered prayers for the members of the royal family. But, after a time, he began to oppress them by levying unjust taxes, and when they refused to pay the taxes he sent an army to punish them.

The Americans then resolved to fight for their rights. In 1775, delegates from the thirteen colonies met at Philadelphia in a Continental Congress. They called for troops and elected George Washington commander-in-chief of the army.

Of course, all the monarchs in Europe were anxious to see how this quarrel between George III and his colonies would end. The French king was more interested than any other. Some people said he would equip a fleet to aid the Americans; yet he was in no haste to adopt such a bold policy as that.

"It would not be wise," he said, "to try to assist those who are too weak to assist themselves;" and he waited to see what George Washington, at the head of the Continental troops, would do.

But one of his courtiers, the Marquis de Lafayette, was not willing to stand idly waiting while the Americans were fighting for their liberties. He said to his friends: "Let us join these patriots in their struggle against the tyranny of an unjust king. We may be defeated; but we shall have the satisfaction of knowing that we have fought on the side of justice and the right."

In the following pages you may read of some of the events in the life of this young French nobleman, who helped to secure the independence of the American Colonies, and afterwards laid the first cornerstone of the present republic of France.

CHAPTER II

THE YOUNG MARQUIS

The château of Chavaniac was in the province of Auvergne, in the south part of France. It was a lofty castle, with towers and narrow windows from which cannon once frowned down upon besieging foes. There was a deep moat around it, with a bridge which was drawn up in time of war, so that no man, on horseback or on foot, could pass in at the gate without permission of the guard.

Château de Chavaniac, Lafayette's Birthplace

Low hills, crowned with vineyards, stood near the castle, and beyond the hills stretched mountains whose peaks seemed to pierce the sky. In all France there was not a more charming spot than Chavaniac; and among all the nobles of the court there was no braver man than its master, the Marquis de Lafayette.

Sometimes the king left the pleasures of his palace to spend a day at this castle; and whenever the young marquis and his beautiful bride went to Paris, they were treated with the greatest respect.

One day, the drawbridge was let down over the moat, and the gallant marquis rode away to the war in Germany. After taking part in several engagements, he was shot through the heart in a skirmish at Minden. His comrades buried him on the field. The drums were muffled, the band played a funeral dirge, and three rounds of musketry announced that the hero's body had been lowered into the grave.

When swift couriers carried the news of his death to Chavaniac, the sorrow of his family and friends was most grievous to see. The castle was like a tomb; the rooms were darkened; and the servants, clad in black, went about on tiptoe, scarcely daring to whisper to one another.

In the midst of this mourning, on September 6, 1757, the only son of the dead marquis was born.

The little orphan was carried to the chapel and christened Marie Jean Paul Roche Yves Gilbert Motier de Lafayette. That seemed a very long name, indeed, for the tiny baby lying so quietly in the good priest's arms; but it was the custom in France to remember distinguished ancestors at a christening, and there were so many of these that the loving mother really thought the name should be longer than it was. She said that his everyday name should be Gilbert.

When Gilbert was old enough, she walked with him instead of leaving him to the care of servants. Sometimes they climbed a high hill to see the sun set over the towers of the château. Then she told him how the de Lafayettes, long before Columbus discovered America, had driven the Arabs from France, and how they had helped to banish the English kings from France, and how his own father had died for the glory of France.

Sometimes, as they walked through the halls of the castle, she showed him the coats-of-mail which his ancestors had worn, and she told him about the swords and banners and other trophies which the de Lafayettes had won in battle.

"I would not have you less brave than they, my son," she would say.

The boy longed for the time to come when he might show his mother how very brave he was. He grew tall and strong, and carried himself like a prince. He wanted to be worthy of his great ancestors.

The year he was eight, there was much excitement about a wolf which prowled in the forest, killing the sheep in the pastures and frightening the peasants nearly out of their wits. Gilbert made this wolf the object of all his walks. He would persuade his mother to sit in some shady spot while he should go a little way into the forest.

"I will return in an instant, dear mamma," he always said; and, lest he might alarm her, he walked quite slowly until a turn in the road hid him from view. Then he marched quickly into the dark wood.

He did this for many days, seeing only frisking squirrels and harmless rabbits. But one morning, as he sped along a narrow path, his eyes wide open and his ears alert to catch every sound, he heard a cracking in the underbrush.

The wolf was coming! He was sure of it. His mind was made up in an instant. He would spring forward quicker than lightning, and blind it with his coat, while with his arms he would choke it to death.

"It will struggle hard," he thought. "Its feet will scratch me; but I shall not mind, and, when all is over, I shall drag it to the feet of mamma, and she will know, and the peasants will know, that I can rid the country of these pests."

He stood listening. His breath came fast. Again he heard the breaking of the bushes. "I ought first to surprise the beast by coming up on it quickly," he whispered.

He tore off his coat, and held it firmly as he hurried on. Soon he saw the shaggy hide, and the great eyes shining through the thicket. He leaped forward with outstretched coat, and—what do you think?—he clasped in his arms a calf that had strayed from the barnyard!

It was a rude shock to the boy. He returned to his mother, who was already alarmed at his absence, and confessed that he had tried to kill the wolf but had found only a calf.

"Ah, you were brave, my son," she said; "I am quite sure that you would have ended the days of that terrible wolf had he but given you the chance."

CHAPTER III

THE COURTIER

When Gilbert was twelve years old, he was sent to school at Paris. His teachers knew how the king had loved his father, and they were very kind, although they did not always give him his own way.

Once, when a prize was offered for the best essay on "A Perfect Horse," he tried to excel. He described a beautiful animal. Its eyes were large and intelligent, and its nostrils trembled with desire to speed away at the first word of its rider; but when the master, instead of speaking gently, raised a whip to strike it, the horse threw him to the ground.

The teacher said that a perfect horse should have been better trained, and gave the prize to a boy whose horse endured the lash of an unjust master.

"I'd rather lose the prize than describe a horse that would tamely submit to injustice," wrote Gilbert to his mother.

He received many letters from his mother telling him how she loved him and how sure she was that he would always do his duty.

One week no letter came; but, instead, the family carriage drew up at the gate of the school. The coachman and footman on the box looked very sad, and his old nurse sat within, crying. She told him his mother was so ill that he must hasten home.

His dear mother died. A few weeks later, his grandfather also died, and he was left sole master of Chavaniac. He was called the "Marquis de Lafayette," and the peasants knelt humbly by the roadside whenever he passed. The king soon sent for him to appear at court, and, when he saw what a fine, manly fellow the young marquis was, he made him a page to the queen.

A few years later, Lafayette became a member of the Royal Guards, and, just about that time, he married the daughter of a powerful duke.

When the old king of France died in 1774, Louis XVI and Marie Antoinette were crowned with much pomp. The young queen was beautiful and gay. The king loved her so dearly that he tried in every way to make her happy. If she wearied of one palace, he called his courtiers together, and, on horseback and in carriages and sedan chairs, they went to another.

Louis XVI

11

His favorite palace was at Versailles, a few miles from Paris. It was in a splendid park, where fountains played and birds sang all day long.

One room in this palace was so large that hundreds of people could dance together in it; and its walls were lined with mirrors in which the lords and ladies might see themselves as they smiled and bowed and danced.

The queen once gave a masquerade ball in this mirror room. The Marquis de Lafayette was there, with his wife. He was dressed in a coat-of-mail which his great-great-grandfather had worn in a war with the Turks.

He was tall, and his face was very pleasant, with its high forehead and clear brown eyes. As he walked down the long room, his wife said to herself: "He is just like a knight of the olden time!" She smiled when she saw him glance into the mirrors. She thought he was a little vain of his good looks.

But the young marquis hardly noticed himself. He was gazing at the shining armor and wondering if he would ever have a chance to fight in a just cause, as his great-great-grandfather had done.

CHAPTER IV

THE DINNER PARTY

The Marquis de Lafayette soon tired of the idle life at Versailles, and, in 1776, when he was just nineteen years old, he went to Metz, a town then in France, as captain of an artillery company.

He was a born soldier. He loved to hear the boom of cannon and the rattle of muskets on the drill ground. The very first time he called off orders to his men, he felt that, if he were only in battle, he could add some glory to his already famous name.

But he said to himself: "Kings make war for conquest. I wish that I might enlist my arms for a more worthy object."

That same year an English nobleman, the royal Duke of Gloucester, chanced to visit Metz. He had displeased his brother, King George III, and for that reason had been banished from England.

The commandant of the garrison gave a dinner-party in honor of the royal guest.

Lafayette and the other French officers were in full uniform; but the Duke of Gloucester was the most splendid of all who sat about the table. There was much laughing and drinking of toasts and speechmaking, until a guard announced that a messenger was at the door with despatches for his royal highness.

"Ah, news from England!" exclaimed the duke.

"Show the man in," ordered the commandant.

A courier, with dust on his garments, entered the room, and, bowing low, delivered a bundle of letters.

"I beg your Highness to read without ceremony," said the commandant.

The duke glanced over the papers for some time in silence. He looked grave. At last, he said: "My courier has brought despatches about our colonies in America."

"Ah," said one; "are the colonies acting badly?"

"Yes, they demand to vote their own taxes."

"How absurd! Why, the people in France do not vote their own taxes."

"You must know," said the duke, "that many years ago, one of the kings of England gave a charter to our people which granted them the right to impose their own taxes. They now elect representatives to a parliament, where they decide how much money should be used by the government. Sometimes, when the king asks for more money than he really needs, they refuse to increase the taxes; but they are usually quite willing to pay whatever he asks."

"What do these Americans complain of, then?" asked Lafayette.

"Taxation without representation," answered the duke. "They insist that, as loyal subjects, they should be allowed either to send representatives to our Parliament, or to have a Parliament of their own. Neither privilege has been granted. Our Parliament imposes taxes on them, and, when they refuse to pay the taxes, the king sends an army to force them to do so. These despatches inform me that the rebels have driven our troops out of a town called Boston, and that delegates from the thirteen colonies have met at another town called Philadelphia and adopted a declaration of independence."

"The rabble!" cried one of the French officers.

"Your fine troops will soon crush the rascals," cried another.

"My brother, the king, is stubborn," said the duke, with a smile. "He banished me, gentlemen, because I disobeyed him. He will conquer these disobedient colonies; but, since our common people are not willing to fight their cousins, he has hired Hessians from Germany to help our soldiers."

A British Soldier

"What, your highness!" exclaimed Lafayette, who could hardly believe that he had heard aright.

"Yes, many thousand Hessians are now on their way across the sea."

Lafayette thought it was cruel for a king to send

a foreign army against his own subjects; but he remembered that the English king was the duke's brother, and he said nothing in reply.

"I am not so sure, gentlemen," said the duke, after a pause; "I am not so sure but the Americans are in the right. They are fighting as freeborn Englishmen."

"The Americans *are* in the right," said Lafayette to himself; and, while the other officers were making merry about many things, he was silent. As soon as he could do so, he excused himself from the table. He hastened to his room and locked the door.

"This is, indeed, the hour I have sought," he murmured.

He sat down to think, and then he arose and paced the floor until it was almost morning. When, at last, he threw himself on the bed to sleep, he had resolved to leave the pleasures of rank and fortune, and even to separate, for a time, from the wife he loved, that he might use his sword in the defense of liberty.

CHAPTER V

THE DEPARTURE FOR AMERICA

As soon as the young captain of artillery could get leave of absence from duty at Metz, he hastened to Paris. Here he found everybody talking of England's war with her colonies.

Now, the French people hardly knew whether Boston was the name of a town or of a whole state; but they were so delighted because the haughty English generals had been defeated there that they had "Boston" whist, and "Boston" tea, and "Boston" snuff.

Lafayette sought out some American agents who were buying arms secretly, and the more he heard about the unjust taxes, the more determined he was to help the patriots resist them.

His father-in-law opposed his plans; but, to strengthen his resolution, Lafayette adopted the motto, "*Cur non?*" which means "Why not?" "*Cur non?*" he said, when he saw his wife in tears. "*Cur non?*" he would say again, when his baby girl stretched out her tiny arms as if to hold him back. With Baron de Kalb, an officer who had been in America, he organized a Boston club, to talk about raising an army.

When Louis XVI heard this, he was displeased. He said that if any French noblemen joined the rebels it might cause England to declare war against France.

Late in the fall, news came of a battle on Long Island, in which the patriots were badly defeated.

"You see," said the king; "those Americans are only a mob. They will soon be disarmed;" and he forbade the meetings of the Boston club.

"Cur non?" said Lafayette; and the meetings were held secretly.

About this time, the American Congress sent Silas Deane, of Connecticut, to France, to seek aid; and Lafayette asked De Kalb to go with him to visit the envoy. When the two men met, they shook hands; but, as neither understood the language of the other, they said nothing.

Baron de Kalb

De Kalb, who could speak both English and French, told Silas Deane that the Marquis de Lafayette wished to join the American army.

"We have no money to pay our officers," said Deane.

"I will serve without money," repeated De Kalb after Lafayette.

"We have no ship to carry you and your men," said Deane.

"I will buy a ship," was the answer.

Still, the American hesitated to accept the services of such a boyish-looking officer.

Silas Deane

Then the modest Lafayette would have blushed if he had understood what his friend said in his behalf. De Kalb told of his wealth and rank, and explained what a powerful ally he might become.

In the end, Silas Deane gave Lafayette a contract to sign, in which Lafayette promised to serve in the army of the United States whenever he was wanted.

When the venerable Benjamin Franklin came to Paris, Lafayette was among the first to greet him. He was enchanted with the famous philosopher, whose simple manners and plain dress befitted well the herald of a republic.

"Now, indeed, is our time of need," said Franklin.

Lafayette waited to hear no more. He bought a ship, and ordered it to be equipped for the long voyage.

While the ship was being made ready, he visited

England, where his uncle was the French ambassador. George III feared that Louis XVI would aid the Americans in their rebellion, and tried to be friendly to France. Lafayette was treated with distinction at court.

He met some English officers who were just ready to start for America, and was invited to Portsmouth to see the ships set sail with troops; but he refused to go.

"I cannot be a hypocrite," he said to himself; "I shall soon have my own ship launched for America."

While at Lord Rawdon's, who had just returned from New York, he heard how General Washington, on a Christmas night (1776), had captured the Hessians at Trenton. He expressed such delight over the news as to arouse suspicion, and, when he found that his movements were watched, he returned to Paris secretly.

The ship was not yet ready. Meantime, George III heard about his plans, and wrote to Louis XVI against the expedition; but, when the letter reached Paris, Lafayette, with De Kalb and eleven other officers, had already set out on his journey.

King Louis sent messengers in pursuit, and then Lafayette disguised himself as a courier, and galloped ahead of his friends to order the relays of horses. In one town, during a wait of three hours, he lay concealed in the straw of a stable. In another town, when he was recognized by the innkeeper's daughter, he made her a sign to be silent just as the pursuers rode up to the door, and she sent them away by a different road.

At last, he reached Pasages, on the Spanish coast, where his good ship *Victory* was anchored. And, when the king's messengers arrived at the edge of the water, all covered with the dust of their swift pursuit, the sails were already spread, and the Marquis de Lafayette was on his way to America.

CHAPTER VI

WASHINGTON'S AIDE-DE-CAMP

The voyage across the ocean was stormy and long. Lafayette spent most of the time trying to learn to speak English.

The *Victory* cast anchor near Charleston, South Carolina, and the party landed about midnight. As Lafayette and De Kalb stood on the beach, they clasped each other's hands, and, looking up to the stars, vowed they would conquer for liberty or die on foreign soil.

They found shelter at a farmhouse, and, on the following day, proceeded to Charleston. Here Lafayette purchased carriages and horses to ride nine hundred miles to Philadelphia, where the Continental Congress was in session. When the carriages broke down because of the bad roads, the officers mounted the horses and continued their journey.

Lafayette could not talk much with the people whom he met, but he soon saw that America was quite different from France. There were no beggars lying by the roadside; the farmers did not kneel when fine carriages passed, and one man really seemed to be just about as respectable as another.

"I am more determined than ever," he said to De Kalb, "to help these people preserve the liberties they have enjoyed."

He reached Philadelphia on July 27, 1777.

Now, King Louis had directed Franklin to write to the Congress requesting it not to give Lafayette a commission in the army; but the shrewd envoy had taken no pains to hurry his letter, and, as it had not been received, Lafayette was given the rank of major general.

The outlook for the Americans was not very encouraging. Washington had retreated from New York, and the British general, Sir William Howe, was preparing to attack Philadelphia.

Lafayette first met Washington in the Quaker City, and knew him at once by his noble face. He had a talk with the commander, who took him to inspect some fortifications, and invited him to cross the Delaware to see his army.

George Washington

When Lafayette arrived at the camp in New Jersey, the troops were on the drill-ground. Many of them were ragged and barefooted. Even the officers lacked suitable uniforms, and the guns were of all shapes and sizes.

"We should be embarrassed at thus showing ourselves to a French officer," said Washington.

"Ah!" replied Lafayette, with tears in his eyes; "men who fight for liberty against such odds will be sure to win."

Washington was so pleased with the modest zeal of the young marquis that he made him one of his aides-de-camp. Lafayette was then just twenty years old.

Another aide of about his age was Alexander Hamilton. Hamilton spoke French almost as well as Lafayette, and the two officers became devoted friends.

Alexander Hamilton

General Howe sailed up Chesapeake Bay, and, landing, marched to attack Philadelphia. Washington, with his army, went to meet him, and there was a terrible battle near Brandywine Creek.

Lafayette was in the thickest of the fight until he was forced to fall back on account of having received a musket ball in the calf of his leg.

"Take care of the marquis as though he were my own son," said Washington to the surgeon.

The Americans were badly defeated at Brandywine, because the British were better disciplined, and had superior arms. Washington retreated, and Philadelphia was taken.

His wound confined Lafayette to his bed for six weeks. During this period of idleness he spent much of the time writing letters to his wife.

"Now that you are the wife of an American general," he wrote, "I must give you a lesson. People in France will say, 'They have been beaten.' You must answer, 'It is true; but with two armies, equal in number and on level ground, old soldiers always have an advantage over new ones; besides, the Americans inflicted a greater loss than they sustained.'

"Then people will say, 'That's all very well, but Philadelphia, the capital of the colonies, is taken.' You will reply, politely, 'You are foolish; Philadelphia is a poor city, open to the enemy on all sides.' "

The devoted little wife repeated these words at court, and thus helped the American cause in France.

When Lafayette was again able to mount a horse, he led an expedition against a post of the Hessians with such skill that he was given command of the Virginia militia.

After some battles around Philadelphia, Washington made his winter quarters at Valley Forge, about twenty miles away; and, while the British were enjoying themselves in the best houses of the Quaker City, the Americans suffered great privations in tents and rude cabins.

This was in the winter of 1777. The weather was very

severe. Some of the soldiers were without shoes, and their feet bled as they walked over the frozen ground; yet, all through the stormy days, the little army drilled and worked on the fortifications, while, at night, those without blankets sat around the camp fires to keep from freezing to death. Lafayette, who had been used to luxuries all his life, willingly shared these hardships, and went limping about from tent to tent with a pleasant word for everybody.

Washington at Valley Forge

Meantime, a British general, Sir John Burgoyne, having attempted to invade New York from Canada, was forced to surrender his whole army to General Gates, at Saratoga.

"You see," said some of the American generals, who were jealous of Washington, "the army in the North is successful; but just look at the army in the South! It has lost Philadelphia, and is only freezing to death at Valley Forge."

These jealous generals plotted to remove Washington from command, and tried in every way to induce Lafayette to favor their evil designs. One night, they invited him to a dinner. After toasts were offered in honor of several officers, Lafayette was grieved to note that the name of Washington had been omitted. He arose to his feet.

"Gentlemen," he cried, "I drink to the health of George Washington, commander-in-chief of the American armies!"

The toast was honored in silence, The treacherous men saw plainly enough that the Marquis de Lafayette would never join in a plot against his general.

CHAPTER VII

LOUIS XVI
PROMISES A FLEET

Now, all this time, Benjamin Franklin was at Paris, working for the colonies. He found that very many of the French people wanted to aid in the war against England.

The noblemen said: "England robbed us of our colonies, we should now seek revenge."

The manufacturers and shopkeepers said: "England never allowed the Americans to buy goods directly from us, and, if we help them win their liberty, we shall get most of their trade."

The wretched peasants did not understand what liberty meant, but they knew all about unjust taxes, and were glad the Americans were refusing to pay them.

But the French king hesitated to send his armies across the sea. He did not believe that the Americans were strong enough to win a single great battle.

"As for helping King George's subjects set up a republic," he said, "that would be a dangerous experiment which my own subjects might wish to try."

Franklin despaired of securing aid from France. One day, as he sat alone, wondering what plan he must next pursue, an American courier arrived from Boston. Franklin met him at the door.

"Sir," he asked, without waiting for the man to speak, "is Philadelphia captured?"

"It is, sir," answered the courier.

Franklin turned sadly away. All seemed lost.

Benjamin Franklin

"But, sir, I have better news than that!" exclaimed the courier, and he showed despatches from Congress which told of the battle of Saratoga, and of Burgoyne's surrender of six thousand men.

Franklin was overjoyed, and hastened to court with the news.

"Really," said the king to himself, "this is the time to give John Bull a fine dose of bitters; these rebels may yet become a great nation." And so he acknowledged the independence of the United States, and promised to send a fleet to America.

CHAPTER VIII

THE FURLOUGH

Lafayette was delighted when he learned that his king had recognized the independence of the United States and had concluded a treaty of alliance.

The event was celebrated on a May day with a grand parade at Valley Forge. There was a salute of thirteen cannon, followed by a volley of musketry, and then the army, drawn up in two lines, shouted: "Long live the king of France!" and gave loud huzzas for the new American States.

A few days later, Lafayette had occasion to show his skill. It happened in this way:

Washington had sent him, with two thousand men, to occupy Barren Hill, half-way between Valley Forge and Philadelphia, and he was directed to fall on the rear of the British if they should attempt to leave the city. He had hardly chosen the camp, near a stone church, with the Schuylkill River on one side and a wood on the other, when spies reported his arrival. The British general, who was attending a grand military ball at Philadelphia, laughed aloud at the news.

"Ha, ha! He, he!" he laughed. "That will make a fine close for our dance." And he went about, saying to the ladies: "I invite you to my house on to-morrow night to meet the Marquis de Lafayette."

Before daylight, nine thousand red-coats were on the march. One division was sent round by a circuitous route to cut off retreat to Valley Forge, while two other divisions approached Barren Hill.

"The little French boy is in a trap," chuckled the British general, as he pushed his way through the mists of the early dawn.

Meantime, scouts brought word to the camp that the "Bloody Backs" were coming. The patriots were in a panic. They ran hither and thither, crying, "All is lost! We cannot escape!"

Lafayette perceived the danger; but he calmed their fears with a jaunty air, and smilingly said: "We will now lead the British a livelier dance than they had last night!"

He had studied the ground and discovered a ford which the enemy knew nothing about. He laid his plans well. He boldly advanced a few columns as if to give battle, and, while the red-coats were preparing to attack them, he hurried the rest of the army across the ford; then he quietly withdrew those who were in the pretended line of battle, and, when the British charged up Barren Hill from opposite sides, they only met one another!

The affair was so very ludicrous that, when the nine

thousand marched back to Philadelphia, they were the sport of everybody.

The British general, hearing that King Louis was sending over a fleet, abandoned the Quaker City. Washington pursued him across New Jersey, and there was a hard-fought battle at Monmouth. In this battle, Lafayette bore himself heroically all day long, and, when night came, with the victory undecided, he slept on the field by the side of Washington.

The enemy retreated to New York, and Washington stretched his lines from Morristown, New Jersey, to West Point, on the Hudson.

While the patriots thus kept watch of New York, Lafayette was granted a furlough. It was thought that he might obtain more aid from France. When he reached Paris, he was placed under arrest; for King Louis had once promised the English ambassador to put the bold young marquis in prison if he should ever return.

And what do you think his prison was?

It was the house of his own family, and the chains that were bound tightly around his neck were the arms of his loving wife.

He was forbidden to enter the king's presence for a week as penance for having disobeyed royal orders; but, at the end of that time, he was again restored to his old place of honor. It is said that the queen and every lady of the court kissed him on both cheeks.

Lafayette turned this whirlwind of favor to the advantage of the patriots. He said that no European army would suffer the tenth part of what the American troops did, and boldly declared that the cost of a single royal ball would equip the whole army.

He talked much about Washington.

"Do you know, Doctor," said the queen one day to Franklin, "that Lafayette has really made me in love with your General Washington? What a man he must be!"

When, at last, Lafayette was ready to return to America, he went in the uniform of an American general to bid the king good-bye. At his side hung a sword, with handle of gold and blade of steel, engraved with his arms and his motto, *Cur non?* It had been presented to him by Franklin in the name of the American Congress.

When he landed at Boston, the bells of the churches rang a welcome, while the citizens marched in line to escort him to General Hancock's house on Beacon Hill.

As soon as he could do so, Lafayette went to army headquarters on the Hudson. There Washington greeted him as if he had been his own son; but he looked anxious and sad.

"Alas, my boy," he said, "there is bad news for you. We have been defeated in the South. Our continental money is so counterfeited by the enemy that it is almost worthless, and our sick and

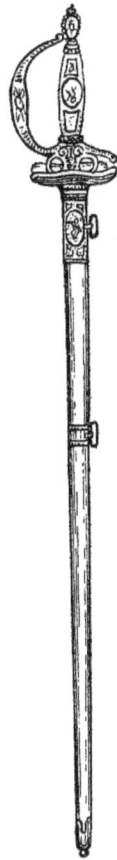

Lafayette's Sword

33

starving soldiers are without supplies."

"Ah!" cried Lafayette, with a joyous laugh, "I have remembered my general during my absence. There are six thousand land troops, under Rochambeau, now on the way, and money, and clothing, and arms."

CHAPTER IX

THE VICTORY AT YORKTOWN

Not long after Lafayette's return, he went with Washington to inspect the fortifications at West Point. While they were there, Washington discovered that Benedict Arnold, the commander of the fort, had been bribed to betray it to the British.

West Point was saved; but Arnold, the traitor, escaped to a British ship, and enlisted in the service of the enemy. This was in September, 1780.

A few months later, Arnold led a British army into Virginia, and Lafayette was ordered south to attack him.

"Look before you leap," were Washington's parting words.

Lafayette remembered the warning, and moved forward with caution. At Baltimore, he borrowed ten thousand dollars from

Benedict Arnold

some merchants to supply his men with shoes and hats, and to buy the linen which the women of the city made into summer garments.

Then he marched to Richmond, Virginia. Arnold soon sent a letter to the camp about an exchange of prisoners. Lafayette said to the messenger: "I will answer the letter of any British officer; but I will not even read a letter from Benedict Arnold, the traitor."

A few days later, the British general, Cornwallis, took command of Arnold's troops.

"The Frenchman cannot escape me!" he said.

The youthful major general warily avoided an engagement with Cornwallis. He joined his forces with those of Anthony Wayne, and followed the British at a distance.

General Anthony Wayne

Some of the best young men of Virginia and Maryland had hesitated to take up arms against the king; but, when they saw the skill and courage of this stranger, they mounted their own horses and joined his ranks. Thus Lafayette's army kept daily increasing.

Now, just at this time, all Europe was awaiting events on two rivers in America. The Hudson, in the

North, lay between Clinton and Washington; and the James, in the South, held on its banks the opposing armies of Cornwallis and Lafayette.

"Whose army will conquer?" was a question which King George and King Louis anxiously asked.

It was not long before they had an answer.

Cornwallis threw up fortifications at Yorktown, and moved his camp there. Then, Washington and Lafayette agreed to unite their armies to attack him.

Soon a French fleet, under Count de Grasse, moved up Chesapeake Bay, and anchored before Yorktown. Lafayette and Wayne marched nearer and nearer, until Cornwallis was surrounded by land and sea.

De Grasse urged Lafayette to make the attack at once. It was a temptation for the young major general. He knew that Europe would ring with his name if he should win the victory alone; but, when he thought of the patient commander in the North, who had borne the burdens of the long war, he said to De Grasse: "No, if we strike the enemy now, our losses will be too great. I shall await the arrival of Washington. To him alone should belong the honor of giving Cornwallis this final blow."

Meanwhile, Washington left the Hudson. Rochambeau, with the French troops, joined him, and together they marched to the South. When the united armies, under the command of Washington, stood in front of Yorktown, Lafayette's division was the first to storm the redoubts.

Cornwallis surren-
dered October 19, 1781;
this ended the war, and
America was free.

Lafayette received
a leave of absence to
return to France. When
he reached Versailles
and found that his wife
was attending a ball at
the palace, he sent her
a message. The tidings
of his arrival ended the

Lord Cornwallis

dancing. Everybody stopped to tell everybody else that
the Marquis de Lafayette had returned from America;
and the queen called her own carriage to accompany
the happy wife home.

Honors were showered on the hero; but he modestly
declared that most of the credit of victory belonged
to Washington. Whenever he dined with the French
officers, he proposed a toast to the health of Washington,
and when his son was born, he named him George
Washington. After the treaty of peace between England
and America had been signed, he wrote to Washington:
"As for you, my dear general, who can truly say that all
this is your work, what must be your feelings!"

Later, he wrote: "The eternal honor in which my
descendants will glory will be to have had an ancestor
among your soldiers."

CHAPTER X

A VISIT TO MOUNT VERNON

In 1784, Lafayette visited Washington at Mount Vernon. The two friends spent many happy days together. They rode after the hounds, or walked on the banks of the Potomac River, or sat in the library musing over the battles they had fought for liberty. They talked much about the thirteen new states, which had not yet formed a permanent union.

Mount Vernon

"There are three things I wish," said Lafayette; "first, that France and America form an alliance; second, that the thirteen colonies be united under one government; and third, that the slaves in the colonies be freed."

Washington agreed with Lafayette about all these measures. The two visited the battlefields of the South, and lingered at the grave of De Kalb, who had fallen at Camden, in South Carolina.

When, at last, Lafayette started north to resign his commission, Washington accompanied him as far as Annapolis. On returning to Mount Vernon, he hastened to write: "In the moment of our separation and every hour since, I have felt all that love, respect and attachment for you with which length of years and your merits have inspired me. I often asked myself, as our carriages separated, whether that was the last sight I ever should have of you."

It was, indeed, the last time they met on earth. Lafayette returned home. He was kept busy for years by important events, and when he again visited America the noble Washington was in his grave.

Perhaps the best service of Lafayette to our country was the good name he gave it in Europe. He also did what he could to improve our trade by finding new markets for our products.

The fishermen of Nantucket were so grateful for his help in the whaling industry that they held a public meeting. Every man present promised two milkings from his cow to make a cheese. Barrels of milk were accordingly collected, and a great round cheese, weighing five hundred pounds, was made; and one day it arrived at Chavaniac, not a whit the less fragrant for its long voyage across the sea. The planters of Virginia were so much pleased with Lafayette's efforts in behalf of the tobacco trade, that they ordered Houdon, the sculptor, to make two marble busts of him. One was placed in the capitol at Richmond, and the other was presented to the city of Paris.

Now, the kings of Europe did not like the new ideas about liberty which had spread over the world after the American revolution. Frederick the Great, of Prussia, invited the Marquis de Lafayette to his court for a visit. In one of their talks, King Frederick said: "By and by, the United States will return to the good old system of monarchy."

Frederick the Great

"Never, sire, never," replied Lafayette; "neither monarchy nor aristocracy can ever exist in America."

"Sir," said Frederick, with a penetrating look, "I knew a young man who, after he had visited countries where liberty and equality reigned, conceived the idea of establishing the same system in his own country. Do you know what happened to him?"

"No, sire."

"He was hanged."

Lafayette looked up with a calm smile; but he did not betray to the anxious king what his thoughts were.

CHAPTER XI

THE NATIONAL ASSEMBLY

It was, indeed, time for the monarchs of Europe to be concerned about the safety of their thrones. Nowhere was the danger greater than in France.

While King Louis had been helping King George's subjects, his own subjects were suffering. They were grievously taxed to support the splendor of the king and his nobles. Whole counties were reduced to starvation, and thousands of wretched creatures wandered over the kingdom, begging or robbing as they went.

Louis XVI saw little of all this misery. He was happy himself, and he wondered why everybody else was not happy. If he chanced to see a pallid face through the window of his coach, he said: "That poor fellow is ill."

No one spoiled his drive by telling him the man was hungry.

The thoughtless king kept asking his ministers for more money, until they told him the treasury was empty. Then the taxes were increased. The people began to hear how the Americans had won the right to vote their own taxes. They asked one another why the French might not have that right too. It really began to look as if there might be a revolution in France.

When Lafayette returned from his visit to Mount Vernon, he advised the king to call an assembly of the nobles to decide what should be done. The assembly was summoned. Lafayette was one of its members. He declared that there must be less extravagance at court instead of more taxes on the workingmen.

"Citizens ought to be allowed to vote their own taxes," he said. "Let us call a national assembly with the common people represented in it."

"What!" cried the other nobles, "would you dare to put that request in writing for the king to read?"

"I dare do anything that may broaden the liberties of my fellowmen," replied the patriot.

He wrote a petition asking that his majesty permit the people of France to elect representatives to help make the laws. He was the only one who was bold enough to sign the paper.

"The marquis will be sent to the Bastille," whispered the nobles to one another, and they expected to see him seized by the guards.

King Louis did not send Lafayette to prison; but he gave no heed to the petition.

Things went from bad to worse until at length the king consented to summon a national assembly to meet at Versailles.

Lafayette represented the nobles of his province and took his seat on May 1, 1789. It was just one day after the inauguration of Washington as President of the United States.

CHAPTER XII

THE FRENCH REVOLUTION

The members of the National Assembly marched in a body to the Church of Saint Louis for prayers. The representatives of the common people walked first, dressed in black; then the noblemen came, in silk and velvet and lace with gold chains about their necks; and last of all came the king and the highest officials of the court.

Thomas Jefferson

It was a magnificent pageant, attended with the clang of trumpets and the chant of priests. The streets were crowded with sight-seers, among whom was Thomas Jefferson, the American minister to France.

Now, the men in black had come from all parts of the kingdom to right the wrongs of the people; yet at the first meeting they heard of nothing but the king's need of more money.

They grew desperate, at last, and boldly declared that there must be better laws. The king listened in silence; then he put on his gold-laced hat; the nobles did the same, and then—what do you think?—the men in black put on their caps!

The king was amazed, and the nobles stared at one another in astonishment; for the common people had never before dared to wear caps in the presence of royalty. But the men in black did not stop at that. They held a meeting among themselves and resolved not to return to their homes until the king had signed a written constitution for the government of France.

Lafayette drew up a Declaration of Rights. It was something like one which the American Congress had sent to George III. Louis XVI agreed to make reforms. Perhaps he tried to do so; but he really did not know how to change the old order of things.

While there were bread riots around the public buildings in Paris, he gave a grand ball at Versailles. Some one hurried to tell the hungry people about it.

"Louis mocks at our misery!" they cried.

And the very next day they stormed the Bastille. They broke down the great doors and set the prisoners free, and then they battered the massive walls to the ground. King Louis was afraid to leave his palace at Versailles.

Electors met in the Hôtel de Ville, or City Hall. They declared there must be a commander of a national guard to keep order in Paris, and when one of them pointed to the bust of Lafayette which Virginia had presented, he was elected by a unanimous vote.

The mobs grew wilder in spite of all the new guard could do. Once when they were raising a gallows upon which to hang a harmless priest, there seemed no way to quell their fury.

The Bastille

Lafayette sprang to a platform. Just then his little boy came to the place with his teacher. He seized the child and held him high up.

"Gentlemen," he said, "I have the honor to present to you my son, George Washington Lafayette!"

The name of the American patriot acted like magic upon the crowds below. Cheers rent the air, and, in the confusion, the poor priest escaped.

As winter came on, food became scarcer than ever. Yet the court at Versailles was feasting. Some one said that when the queen heard the people had no bread, she laughingly asked: "Why don't they eat cake then?" and that a nobleman said: "Nay, let them eat grass!"

The rage of the mobs increased. Lafayette stationed the National Guard on the road to Versailles to prevent them from going there. But one day a fish-woman beat a drum. The ragged and hungry people ran together, and soon thousands were on their way to Versailles.

"Bread! Bread!" they cried.

The guard gave way. The mad creatures reached the palace. They killed the Swiss guards at the doors and ran their pikes into the queen's empty bed.

Lafayette had followed swiftly with the National Guard. He drove the intruders from the palace and talked to them until they seemed more calm.

Then he led Louis to the balcony above them.

"Long live the king!" they shouted.

"Come," said Lafayette to Marie Antoinette. She appeared with the little prince and the princess.

"Not the children!" "Not the children!" they cried; for they did not wish the innocent to suffer.

The terrified queen sent the children within. She stood on the balcony alone. She expected instant death.

Lafayette stepped forward. He bowed low and kissed her hand. The people again forgot their anger.

"Long live the queen!" "Long live the general!" they shouted as they beat their pikes together.

"Perhaps things would mend if their majesties left

this costly palace," said a grimy blacksmith to a thin-visaged tailor.

"They must go to Paris!" screamed the tailor.

"On to Paris!" was the cry from a thousand throats.

The royal family was forced into a carriage. It was a strange procession that went back into the great city. Lafayette and the guard rode on each side of the splendid carriage, but, before and behind, marched men and women with wild eyes and unkempt hair. Some held on their

Queen Marie Antoinette

pikes the pillaged loaves of bread, and others the bloody heads of the Swiss guards, while the fish-woman led the van with her drum.

At last, their majesties were safe in the palace at Paris. Lafayette had rescued them from death; yet he was firm in his devotion to the liberties of the people. He said to the National Assembly: "If the king will sign a constitution for the just government of France, I shall defend him; if he refuses to sign, I will fight him."

Soon after this Louis signed a constitution which was much like that of England. On July 14, 1790, the anniversary of the fall of the Bastille, the French celebrated the beginning of their freedom. In an open field where thousands of the people had assembled, the king and the members of the new assembly pledged to support the constitution.

When Lafayette ascended the steps to take the oath, in the name of the army, there was loud applause; and, as he rode at the head of the National Guard in the parade which followed the solemn ceremony, all eyes were fixed on him.

In his joy at what seemed to be the end of tyranny in his native land, he sent to Washington the key to the fallen Bastille, where men had once been imprisoned for life without trial by jury. To-day, you may see the great iron key among the historic treasures of Mount Vernon.

CHAPTER XIII

AN EXILE AND IN PRISON

The French people had not yet learned the first lesson in self-government. The constitutional monarchy soon failed. Mobs imprisoned the royal family and set fire to the houses of the nobles.

Lafayette was grieved over these events. He had led the enslaved people toward liberty, but as soon as they were free they had outrun their guide. Because he would not join them in their excesses, they called him an aristocrat and threatened him with death.

He fled from Paris and wrote to his wife to join him in England. "Let us go to America," he said, "and establish ourselves there. Some day, when the storm is over, I may yet serve France."

But the monarchs of Europe said: "This Marquis de Lafayette, who brought these outrageous ideas of liberty from America, must be silenced."

He was arrested on the frontier and imprisoned in Prussia for a year. Then he was sent to a dungeon at Olmutz in Austria. He had wretched food. His clothes rotted with dampness. His bed was a pile of straw. Yet when he was told he might be free if he would betray the military strength of France, he refused to leave his cell. He expected to die in his chains.

One morning he heard a rattle of keys and bars. He arose from his straw and saw his wife and two daughters enter beneath the crossed swords of the guards. The joy was too great. He fell in a swoon. When he recovered his senses, he tenderly embraced his loved ones.

"And where is my little George?" he asked.

"He is at Mount Vernon with Washington," replied his wife.

"God be praised for such a friend in our hour of need," exclaimed the now happy father.

When he was strong enough to bear it, the Marquise told him what had happened at Paris. It was a sad story.

The king and queen had been beheaded; her own

James Monroe

grandmother, mother, and sister, with thousands of others, had been led to the scaffold during a reign of terror. She herself had been in prison until released through the efforts of James Monroe, the new American minister to France. After many trials she had obtained permission to share his captivity.

The devoted wife remained at Olmutz.

Meanwhile, Washington, Jefferson and other friends appealed to the Austrian emperor to set the patriot free.

"It is impossible," replied the despot. "Lafayette's existence is a menace to the kingdoms of Europe."

When, at last, Napoleon Bonaparte, at the head of his French troops, defeated the allied powers, who were trying to place another king upon the throne of France, he refused to sign a treaty of peace until all the French prisoners were surrendered.

Lafayette was liberated. He went to Hamburg, in Germany, with his wife and daughters. His son returned from America, and the united family lived for a time in exile.

Napoleon Bonaparte

When Napoleon became First Consul of France, he pledged himself to restore the constitution for which Lafayette had struggled so long. The patriot then returned to his native land. Most of his property at Chavaniac had been confiscated, and he made his home at La Grange, in the province of La Brie.

La Grange, Home of Lafayette

Formerly the peasants on his estates had knelt when he passed. The revolution had changed all that; but when he taught them self-respect, they showed respect for others without servility.

The Americans did not forget Lafayette in his retirement. In 1805, President Jefferson offered to appoint him governor of Louisiana; but his wife's health was too feeble to permit of the long voyage.

Two years later the noble wife died. At her own request she was buried in that part of the cemetery of Picpus which is called the "cemetery of the beheaded," because there lay the bodies of her relatives who had fallen victims to the mobs.

Napoleon did not keep his pledges to obey the constitution. He made himself emperor of France. After a time he was exiled by the allied powers of Europe, and Louis XVIII was placed on the throne.

Lafayette was a member of the National Assembly for several years, trying always to preserve the liberties of the people. Then he retired to La Grange, where he expected to live quietly with his children for the rest of his days.

CHAPTER XIV

THE MAN OF TWO WORLDS

In 1824, in accordance with a resolution of Congress, President James Monroe invited Lafayette to visit the United States. He gladly accepted the invitation, and set out on his journey with his son George Washington and a private secretary.

"It has been thirty years since I last saw the people of America," he said to himself. "I must be prepared to meet indifferent glances; for most of my friends have long since passed away."

He expected to land quietly in New York and secure private lodgings; but when he arrived he found that he was the nation's guest.

The city was having a holiday in his honor. Thousands stood on the wharves to greet him, while cannon roared and banners waved.

"WELCOME, LAFAYETTE!" was inscribed on the arches beneath which he passed, and his portrait, stamped on blue ribbon, was everywhere to be seen.

Lafayette now understood that he had not been forgotten, and his eyes overflowed with tears.

As he went about from city to city, he aroused the greatest enthusiasm.

He limped a little as he walked. The people said it was because of the wound he had received at Brandywine, and their gratitude seemed without bounds. In one public procession was the model of a ship with his youthful pledge: "I will purchase and equip a vessel at my own expense."

In another a chorus of white-robed girls sang:

"We bow not the neck and we bend not the knee,
But our hearts, Lafayette, we surrender to thee."

Statue of Lafayette,
Union Square, N. Y.

It all seemed like the close of a fairy story where the armed knight, who had once rushed to the rescue of young America in distress, returned again after many years to behold her golden days of prosperity.

The thirteen small colonies had become twenty-four united states; the population had grown from three millions to twelve millions; towns had become cities; forests had been transformed into farms; and the ships, which sailed on every sea, carried the products of soil and loom and forge to the markets of the world.

When, from the well-filled public treasury, Congress presented two hundred thousand dollars to the hero, he received the gift with touching words of gratitude; but when the legislatures of Virginia, Maryland, and other states began to vote large sums of money for him, he firmly refused to accept of their generosity.

He stood at the tombs of Washington, Hamilton, Franklin, and other soldiers and statesmen who had helped to establish liberty, and he visited Jefferson and John Adams, whose tottering footsteps had almost reached the grave, to learn from their lips the story of the new republic.

John Adams

On June 17, 1825, the anniversary of the battle of Bunker Hill, Lafayette assisted in laying the cornerstone of the Bunker Hill monument.

Many thousand people came to Boston to witness the ceremonies. During an eloquent address, Daniel Webster turned to the French patriot. "Fortunate, fortunate man!" he exclaimed; "you were connected with both hemispheres and with two

Daniel Webster

generations! Heaven saw fit that the electric spark of liberty should be conducted through you from the New World to the Old, and we, who are now here to perform this duty of patriotism, have all of us long ago received it from our fathers to cherish your name and your virtues.

"Those who survived the battle of Bunker Hill are now around you. Some of them you have known in the trying scenes of war. Behold them now stretch forth their feeble arms to embrace you! Behold, they raise their trembling voices to invoke the blessings of God on you and yours forever!"

Bunker Hill Monument

On July 4th, Lafayette was at New York and listened to the reading of the Declaration of Independence.

Well did he remember the dinner party at Metz, nearly fifty years before, where he had first heard about this Declaration of Independence. And as he sat upon a high platform and looked down upon the thousands before him, he smiled in content, for he thought he saw in their happy faces the fulfilment of his youthful dreams. Yet a few weeks later he began to fear for the safety of the Republic.

There was a tremendous uproar during a political campaign for the election of the next President. At the taverns, on busy streets and lonely roads, in every nook and cranny of the country, people disputed about whether Andrew Jackson, Henry Clay, John Quincy Adams, or William H. Crawford would make the best President.

Public opinion was so divided that when election day came no candidate received a majority of votes. The Frenchman thought that there really seemed no way to settle the result except with pistols and swords.

He did not know much about the laws of the United States. But he soon learned what a great instrument of good government our Constitution is.

The Constitution provides that when no candidate has received a majority of the electoral votes, the three highest names on the list must come before the House of Representatives.

When, at last, John Quincy Adams was chosen by the House, all factions accepted the verdict.

"Ah!" exclaimed Lafayette, "this is, indeed, a wonderful nation. It is built on a solid foundation, and cannot fall."

The more he traveled in the United States, the more he was impressed with the greatness of its future. When he sailed up the Mississippi and the Ohio and saw the rude cabins on their banks, he said: "These are the beginnings of cities."

When he drove over the National Pike Road or made a voyage on the new Erie Canal, he said: "These are the beginnings of yet greater highways which will one day unite"—Do you think he said the Atlantic Ocean with the Pacific Ocean? No, he did not say that, because in 1825 the Mexicans claimed most of the territory west of the Rocky Mountains. He said—"which will one day unite all sections of the country."

Lafayette spent more than a year with his friends. When his visit was over, he embarked in a new American frigate, the *Brandywine,* and the prayers of millions followed him as he sailed away for the last time from our shores. So much honor had been shown this guest of the nation that, for many years after, if any one received special attention, he was said to be "Lafayetted."

Nor was the hero forgotten in his absence. Old places in the East and new places in the West and South remembered him until, to-day, there are over ninety towns and counties in the United States whose names recall him or the home of his old age.

The boys and girls who are so fortunate as to live at La Grange, or Lafayette, or Fayetteville, or Fayette Hill, or any other Fayette, must surely think often of the gallant young French marquis who came to the rescue of our thirteen struggling colonies.

CHAPTER XV

THE LAST DAYS
OF A PATRIOT

When Lafayette arrived in France he was received
with open arms by his countrymen. They called him
the protector of their Constitution. And, indeed, just at
that time the French Constitution needed protection.

During Lafayette's absence Louis XVIII had died
and Charles X had come to the throne. King Charles
was determined to restore the old order of things. He
destroyed the liberty of the press, dissolved the National
Assembly, and chose his favorites as ministers.

The members of the Assembly met again of their
own accord, and declared they would resist these
unconstitutional measures. Then the people of Paris
rushed together. They barricaded the streets, defeated
the royal troops, and drove the king from the city.

Lafayette might have been elected President, but he
refused to accept the office; for he knew very well that
the French people were not ready for a republic. He
desired a constitutional monarchy like that of England.
He visited Louis Philippe, the Duke of Orleans. This
prince had traveled in the United States and England,

and understood what a government "by the people, for the people" meant.

"You know," said Lafayette to the duke, "that I regard the Constitution of the United States as the most perfect that has ever existed."

"I think as you do," replied his highness; "it is impossible to have passed two years in America and not be of that opinion. But do you believe that the French people are ready for that?"

"No, they are only ready for a throne surrounded with republican institutions."

"Such is my belief," said the duke.

Soon after this the National Assembly met in the Hotel de Ville. The Duke of Orleans was there. He pledged himself to receive the crown, not by right of birth, but as the free gift of the people.

Lafayette led him to an open window and embraced him.

"Long live the Duke of Orleans!" shouted the people who had assembled below to greet him.

Not long after, he was crowned King of France by the Assembly.

"Long live King Louis Philippe!" cried every one.

Louis Philippe

Lafayette felt that he had at last won his long fight for the constitutional liberty of his beloved country. The aged patriot retired to La Grange, where he lived yet a little longer among his children and friends. In his favorite room hung the portraits of Washington and Franklin and a painting of the siege of Yorktown; and here he loved to sit and muse over the exciting scenes of his early days.

One beautiful morning, May 20, 1834, he died at Paris, surrounded by his family; and there was mourning throughout France: His remains were placed with great pomp by the side of those of his wife in the cemetery of Picpus. As the casket was lowered, earth from America, mingled with that of France, was strewn upon it.

Lafayette's Grave

"Lafayette was a man of two worlds," said the Paris papers which were banded in black.

Church bells tolled in his honor in many countries. In the United States, Congress wore mourning for thirty days, and, by order of President Jackson, the same honors were paid to his memory by the army and navy as had been paid to that of George Washington.

As the years went by, the French people learned to govern themselves. They created a republican government, and to-day the Republic of France is one of the great powers of Europe.

As for the United States, the government has grown steadily stronger and greater upon the foundations which Lafayette helped to build.

It was Washington who said: "Lafayette deserves all the gratitude which our country can render him."

And on October 19, 1898, the anniversary of the victory at Yorktown, young patriots in every city, town, and village in our country remembered these words. They held memorial services in Lafayette's honor, and contributed funds to erect, in the city of Paris, a noble monument to his name. And all agreed that the monument should be dedicated on July 4, 1900, the anniversary of our Declaration of Independence.

For it was the news of Liberty's birth which first taught the young captain of artillery at Metz what his mission in life should be.

Liberty Enlightening the World

Presented by the People of France
to the Republic of the United States

www.ingramcontent.com/pod-product-compliance
Lightning Source LLC
LaVergne TN
LVHW011412080426
835511LV00005B/491